*Hiring*
*for*
*Information Technology Positions*

*By*
*Missy Rennet*

*A handbook of semi-technical screening*
*questions for recruiters and HR professionals*

# Table of Contents

# Preface

*The questions in this book are a helpful supplement to the first round of recruiting for IT professionals so you can identify qualified individuals to present to the hiring manager, deep technical screener or interview panel. Incorporating these questions can get your conversation going and allow you to assess how fluent your candidate can speak to his/her profession as well as provide you with a feeling as to their depth of experience. Many of these questions relate to the technical role itself and so can be used regardless of trending products. With the dynamic and swift pace of technology, obviously questions pertaining to the job requirements still need to be asked. Many of the questions in the book can also be tailored to substitute the technologies in your job description.*

# 1 Business Analyst

*A "BA" understands the entire system from both user and developer perspectives and acts as a liaison between these groups.*

1. What techniques do you use to gather requirements?

You want to hear that a variety of techniques are used. Some examples are JAD (joint application design) sessions, surveys, reviewing existing documents, one on one interviews and job shadowing.

2. Can you give me some examples of various requirements models?

Some examples are data flow diagram, process flow diagram, context diagram, sequence diagram, user interface flows, decision trees.

3. What are functional requirements and nonfunctional requirements?

Functional requirements are features that must be included in a system to meet business needs such as business rules, audit tracking, or authentication level. Think in terms of what the system should provide or do for the user. Non-functional requirements are qualities the systems must have such as reliability, scalability, maintainability, speed and platform.

4. What is a traceability matrix?

This tracks requirements from concept to implementation to test to fulfillment. It provides backward and forward traceability, it links requirements, design specifications, test requirements and code files and it serves as a type of map to locate information.

5. What is a Use Case and a User Story?

A Use Case focuses on how the system interacts with other systems and with people. It is very detailed and can be written by an individual or a group of people. It traditionally requires someone to sign off on it and it can take days to author and obtain sign off. It is used in more traditional software development methodologies such as Waterfall.

A User Story is a simple description of a requirement that covers who wants what and why and it can be written on an index card. This brief description promotes a conversation among the team to understand the details which are then confirmed, tested and validated. It is a component of the Agile software development methodology.

6. What are your steps in User Acceptance Testing and what UAT documents have you created?

UAT is the process of the users testing the functionality of the feature to verify it will satisfy their need and work as they requested.

A Business Analyst may: identify test scenarios; create the user acceptance test plan which outlines which test validates which deliverable; create test cases, which are the steps to guide the user; run some tests themselves; record the test results, document any defects that need to be fixed and confirm that the business objective was delivered successfully.

7. What relational database management systems (RDBMS) have you been exposed to and can you write simple SQL queries?

Oracle, MySQL, Microsoft SQL Server, IBM DB2, SAP Hana, Teradata are some popular examples. Most systems work in conjunction with a relational database and it can be useful for a Business Analyst to query a new system during the testing phase or if the company uses an automated system for managing the requirements the BA can use SQL queries to analyze the information.

8. What tools have you used to create visualization documents?

Examples are Unified Modeling Language (UML) or Microsoft Visio. UML is used to visualize the design of a system and MS Visio is used for flow charting a process or a swim lane. (A swim lane covers who does what process, including shared processes. They can be vertical or horizontal)

9. What documents have you created?

Some examples are business requirement document, functional specification document, wireframes, prototype, traceability matrix, test cases, system requirement specifications, product backlog

10. What types of projects have you worked on?

Some examples might be web application development, software development, a system update for processing large volume of transactions or claims, new product development for financial or insurance offerings, mainframe decommissioning, moving to the cloud, implementing new security feature or process, marketing, e-commerce, compliance auditing.

11. What project methodologies have you worked in?

Some answers could be Waterfall, Agile, a blend of both, Scrum, Rapid Application Development (RAD), Six Sigma, Lean, Prince2, Prism.

# 2 Project Manager

*A "PM" is a leader and agent of change responsible for keeping all the elements of a project together by coordinating time, budget and resources and delegating tasks across the team.*

1. What project management methodologies are you most familiar with?

Some examples are Waterfall, Agile, a blend of both, Scrum, Rapid Application Development (RAD), Six Sigma, Lean, Prince2, Prism.

2. How do you start a project?

Understand vision and objectives, identify stakeholders, identify client expectations and commitments, identify dependencies and risks, layout plan, develop a project charter with milestones.

3. How do you manage risk?

This varies and could involve multiple steps: listing what could happen and determine the impact; determine the risk probability; rank the risk lowest to highest; develop mitigation strategies and contingency plans

4. What tools and techniques do you use to monitor and control projects?

Some examples are budget tracking, resource plan, communication plan, issues management and escalation management.

5. What is the largest project you have been managed in terms of: time, budget amount and team size?

6. Do you have experience creating a budget?

7. What project documentation have you created?

Some examples include charter, scope statement, communication plan, change requests, requirements document, status updates, cost estimate, issue log, and closeout report

8. What types of projects have you managed?

Examples are infrastructure, software development, application development, software implementation, security, compliance, moving to cloud and system decommissioning.

9. What would you say is your management style?

# 3 Help Desk Analyst

*A person who provides technical support for the information system users including computer hardware, operating systems, software applications, networks and connectivity.*

1. Which Windows Operating Systems do you have experience supporting?

2. What is the size of the biggest network you have supported in terms of number of users, number of servers and number of locations?

3. What is your experience with:
Troubleshooting connectivity to a virtual private network (VPN)?
Mobile device support?
Printer support?

4. What ticketing systems have you used?

5. How many tickets have you processed on average on a daily basis?

6 What software applications have you supported?

7. What mobile devices and personal digital assistants (PDA) have you supported?

8. Do you have experience removing malware and if so what steps did you take?

You want to hear that they have disconnected from the internet. You do not want to hear that they take a back-up, as that would include backing up the virus. Other things to listen for include operating in safe mode and running a virus scan.

9. What does DHCP mean and what is its purpose?

Dynamic Host Configuration Protocol. It allows a server to automatically assign a different IP (internet protocol) address to a computer from a fddefined range of numbers (already configured for a given network). each time that computer is logged on to the internet. This is called a dynamic IP address.

10 Have you ever done PC imaging or re-imaging and if so what tools did you use?

11. What remote software have you used to log in to users' computers?

12. What levels of support have you provided?

Level 1 is the front line, the first person to try to provide the solutions. If the Level 1 analyst cannot provide the solution it moves to Level 2 and finally Level 3.

# 4 Network Administrator

*A Network Admin installs, configures and supports local area networks (LAN), wide area networks (WAN) and virtual private networks (VPN.)*

1. What is the size of the network you currently work on and what was the largest (number of nodes (connection point) or largest number of servers, workstations, printers, virtual users)?

2. What operating systems do you have experience with?

Some answers could be Unix, Linux, Windows

3. What tools do you use to run diagnostics?

4. What is a switch, a router and a firewall?

All are tangible, physical objects.
A switch connects multiple computers and mobile devices together to form a local network.

A router connects separate physical or logical networks, allowing information to route from one to the other.

A firewall is a security device that puts up a barrier between a local network and the Internet.

5. What brands of routers, switches and firewalls are you familiar with and what has been your experience with each?

Brands could be Cisco, Palo Alto, Juniper or others easily found by a quick internet search and experience could be installing, configuring and troubleshooting.

6. What do you use for scripting/automating and what are some tasks you have automated?

Some examples of what is used to write automation are bash or shell or Perl scripting, Python, Ansible, Puppet and Chef. Scripting /mini programming is employed to automate various network administration tasks that are performed daily or multiple times a day or maybe occasionally but involve a large number of servers that are geographically separated. These tasks will vary and could relate to device provisioning, storage or log on activities.

7. What protocols and topologies do you work with?

Protocols are standards that define the method of

transmitting data. The list of protocols is long and could be found online. A few are listed below by type.

Application layer protocols for the Internet - HTTP, FTP and TCP

Wireless network protocols - WIFI, Bluetooth and LTE

Network routing protocols - EIGRP, BGP and OSPF

Data link layer protocols - PPTP and LT2P

Session layer protocols - DNS and LDAP

Transport layer protocols - TCP, Mobile IP

There are physical topologies which are the pattern the nodes and lines of a network are connected and there are logical topologies which describe how signals act, how data flows, on the network.

The basic topologies are: ring, star, bus, mesh, tree, point to point, daisy chain, hybrid.

# 5 Security Analyst

*This InfoSec role typically comes in 3 levels and there are also several specialties within the realm of security but at the basis is protection from data loss and service interruptions.*

1. Where are your daily news checks from?

2. How do you go about securing a server?

This will vary but listen for giving a user only essential privileges to perform their job, secure passwords, configure firewall rules for remote access, audit the services running on the server and verify their legitimacy, audit the files on the server.

3. What is DNS monitoring and what tools have you used?

It is using monitoring tools to keep tabs on your authoritative domain name server. They test the connectivity between the DNS and your local servers.

4. How do you remediate a desktop that has been attacked?

Disable all network connections including the

internet. Pull the hard drive out and connect it to another computer as a secondary non-bootable driver. Run a malware scan. Make a back-up and rescan it. Return the drive to its original computer. Completely wipe the infected hard drive even if scanning indicated the threat is gone. Reload the operating system. Reinstall security software. Reload the backed-up data. Make a complete back-up of the clean system.

5. Have you ever participated in a vulnerability assessment and if so what did you do?

There are tools that can run a scan and identify every computer by IP address and their associated vulnerabilities such as missed patches. This list gets reviewed and importance should be assigned to each resource to prioritize fixes.

6. Have you ever participated in a security audit and if so what was your responsibility?

The audit consists of a criteria checklist of things to be in place or to be done to ensure company compliance to their security policy. It could include a great variety of items such as change control, regular review of firewall configurations, back-up and restore plans. Many lists need to be generated to prepare for an audit such as IP addresses, applications used and external security devices.

# 6 Quality Assurance Analyst

*A QA Analyst tests the software or website to make sure it functions correctly.*

1. What is a test case?

It describes the step by step process to test a specific function.

2. What is a test plan?

It is a document that describes the scope, approach, resources and schedule of intended testing activities. It identifies the features to be tested, the testing tasks and who will be performing them.

3. What is a test strategy?

It is a document that describes the test efforts, test configuration, testing tools to be employed, the test environment, what types of tests will be carried out and entry and exit criteria.

4. What is smoke testing?

It is a preliminary test to check that the major functionalities are not broken.

5. What is the difference between load testing and performance testing?

Performance testing checks that the application will perform well under its expected load and it checks things like speed, stability and maximum users. Load testing steadily increases the demands on the application and finds its threshold.

6. What is regression testing?

When new functionality is added or when bugs are fixed, regression testing makes sure these changes have not broken other parts.

7. Have you performed automated testing, if so how much and what tools have you used?

In automated testing software tools execute pre-scripted tests, report outcomes and compare results with earlier test runs. Some popular tools are Selenium, HP Quality Center, HP LoadRunner, SilkTest, IBM Rational Functional Tester, Cucumber, Xamarin, LoadStorm.

8. What is manual testing best suited for?

Ofcourse when test cases are executed manually without any support from tools or scripts, time and human error come into play but there are times when human skills cannot be replaced by technology. Exploratory testing, which requires the creativity, intuition and analytical skills of the tester is a good use for manual testing. Likewise, usability testing, which measures how convenient and friendly the product is, requires human observation. Ad-hoc testing is unplanned and calls for the insight and understanding of the tester.

# 7 Database Administrator

*A DBA performs tasks that support and maintain the database(s) and ensures data integrity and security.*

1. What databases and versions do you have the most experiences with?

There is a great variety, some more common names include: Microsoft SQL Server, Oracle, IBM DB2, MySQL, Teradata, MongoDB, PostgreSQL and they all have a number of versions such as Microsoft SQL Server 2016 or Oracle Database 11g. There are differences among these and someone fluent in one will not hit the ground running on a different database.

2. What is a non-relational database and a relational database and what is your experience with each?

Non-relational databases (categorized as NoSQL) are designed to handle unstructured data that doesn't fit neatly into rows and columns, such as Big Data. Big Data grows and moves fast and is very diverse (think of fraud detection or consumer purchasing trends).

The relational database (RDB) contains data that is neatly organized into tables with records (the records are rows) and columns. (think of sales where you have a salesperson, a customer, an item, purchase order and historical purchases).

3. What is the size of the database(s) you have worked on (amount of data it holds)?

The data unit of measures from lowest to highest are: bit (b), byte(B), kilobyte(KB), megabyte(MB), gigabyte(GB), terabyte(TB), petabyte(PB), exabyte(EB), zettabyte(ZB) yottabyte(YB).

4. Do you have experience in ERP environments?

Obviously, this is a Yes/No question but you are trying to ascertain experience with size and complexity. The main feature of an ERP system is a shared database that supports multiple functions and is used by different business units.

5. Have you ever participated in a database conversion and if so what were the technologies and what tasks did you perform?

6. What database tasks do you perform on a regular basis?

Installing the database software, capacity

planning, performance monitoring and tuning, load balancing, backup and recovery, patching the database server, manage users and security by setting up user accounts to control logins to the database (authentication); setting permissions on various parts of the database (authorization); tracking who did what with the database (auditing)

7. What is replication?

It is a backup method for real-time automated backups between multiple database servers. This allows for the creation of either a fall-over server, or warm backup to use in case the main server goes down.

8. What is normalization?

It is a technique for improving performance. Data is split off into tables of specific topics with columns that pertain to or support that topics. Smaller queries can then be run on individual tables instead of having everybody always 'talking' to the entire database — thus improving performance.

9. Have you been involved in high level business planning sessions?

10. Have you worked with a data warehouse development team and if so what were some tasks associated with that?

# 8 UX Designer

*User Experience (UX) Designers are responsible for the ease of use and enhancing customer satisfaction and loyalty by improving usability and the pleasure provided in the interaction between the user and the product.*

1. What is your design process?

This may vary per situation but components in order are:
User research, creating user personas and user flows, prototyping (also known as wireframing), execution which will involve coordinating with User Interface Designers, Developers and integration, validating features and finally metrics and analytics.

2. What design tools do you use the most?

Wireframing and prototyping: Invision, Axure, Balsamiq, Mockplus are some common software tools

UI (user interface) design: Adobe Photoshop, Adobe Illustrator, Sketch are common.

Collaboration: Realtime Board and Slack are currently popular applications.

3. How do you decide which features to incorporate?

(Of course this answer will vary, and it will vary depending on if a new product is being developed or if a modification is being made.
This is a good question to ascertain soft skills and passion.) Some answers to listen for will include research, knowing who the user is, user goals, and asking 'what problem does it solve?'.

4. How much experience do you have conducting concept and usability testing and gathering feedback?

5. What types of metrics have you had to analyze? Some answers are usage data such as time on task, traffic patterns, conversions, outcomes.

6. What front end technologies are you knowledgeable in?

An understanding of front end technologies such as HTML CSS, JavaScript can be useful for the UX Designer.

# 9 UI Designer

*The User Interface Designer creates the look and presentation of the product.*

1. What principles of UI design do you find most helpful?

Know your audience, reduce clutter, use color and contrast, consistency, establish visual hierarchy, proper use of typeface are a few of the main ones.

2. What are some of the trending UI technologies and which do you know?

At the time of this writing they are: Angular JS, ES6, React, backbone.js. HTML5, CSS3, jQuery, Bootstrap.

3. Give me some examples of graphical elements you have incorporated. Vector, infographics, floral, hipster.

4. What content management systems do you know?

WordPress, Drupal, Joomla and Magento are just a few of the many.

# 10 Web Developer

*A programmer who develops applications that are run over the internet from a web server to a web browser.*

1. Are you equally proficient in server side and client-side development?

2. What are your top 3 technologies?

Client side and front-end technologies include HTML, JavaScript, CSS, AJAX, and more
 Server-side technologies could be Java, ASP.net, PHP, Python, C#.net and others.

Note: back end refers to the functionality residing in the background of a site and could include RESTful web services, a database, scripts to process requests to pull out data, an API structure to exchange data, or auto scaling to support load changes.

3. What are some ways you have reduced the load time of a web application?

Answers could include: enable browser caching, reduce redirects, enable compression, optimize images, optimize CSS delivery, reduce the number of plugins, minify code

4. What is a SPA?

A single page application which interacts with the user by dynamically re-writing the webpage instead of loading entire new pages from the server.

5. What are popular SPA technologies?

Mongo, Express, AngularJS, NodeJS ReactJS.

6. What experience do you have integrating applications with third-party APIs (Application Programming Interfaces)?

SOAP, REST, WSDL, are examples of web services. Web service is any piece of software that makes itself available over the internet or in other words the means by which devices communicate on the world wide web. Web services use the internet to provide application to application interaction.

# 11 Full-Stack Developer

*A full-stack developer has broad knowledge of technologies in front and back end development technologies and server administration, with some specialties in a few of the concepts and technologies.*

1. What frameworks and programming languages are you strongest in?

Frameworks provide a lot of the groundwork so you don't need to code every single thing from scratch. There are many and this is an ever-evolving area. At the moment more popular ones include Angular JS framework or Backbone framework or ReactJS framework for the JavaScript language. Rails is the framework for the language Ruby, CakePHP is a framework for PHP, Django is a framework for Python, Hibernate, Springs and Struts are all frameworks for the Java programming language while .Net (dot net) and entity are frameworks for the languages C#.net, VB.net and ASP.net MVC.

2. What scripting languages do you know?

Scripting languages are a simple way to automate a task and typically do not need to be compiled, they simply execute at runtime. An example of use is when you click on Contact Us and your email form opens up with an email address in the To.

3. What databases have you stored data in and accessed data from?

SQL Server, NoSQL, Oracle, MySQL, DB2, MongoDB

4. What server management tasks are you experienced in?

Connecting to the remote servers, managing user groups, permissions and firewalls on the server, install and upgrade software.

5. What Cloud platforms are you experienced working with and have you ever migrated an application from a traditional server to the Cloud?

At the moment Amazon Web Services (AWS), Microsoft's Azure and Google Cloud are the 3 most popular public cloud platforms. Clouds can also be private.

# 12 Artificial Intelligence

*AI is the computer science of building computers or systems able to perform tasks commonly associated with intelligent beings.*

1. What is the difference between applied AI and general AI?

General AI is the building of systems that think and function as the human mind does while applied replicates the reasoning of human intelligence for a single purpose.
Examples of applied AI include systems designed to trade stocks intelligently or operate an automobile without a driver or recommend a song when you select a music genre. Furthermore, general AI is still an emerging field and at this publishing, there is not a computer that can function with the capabilities of even a 6-year-old human, whereas applied AI has been successfully in use for many years.

2. What is top-down parsing?

A strategy of looking first at the highest level of the parse tree and working down, analyzing unknown data relationships by hypothesizing general tree structures and comparing compatibility with the known fundamental structures.

3. What is meant by AI neural networks?

They mathematically model the manner the human brain works which makes machines capable of recognizing speech and images.

4. What is the difference between statistical AI and classical AI?

Statistical induces a thought based on a set of patterns whereas classical AI deduces a conclusion from a set of constraints. Currently statistical AI tends to be programmed in C++ language while classical is programmed more often using LISP.

5. What is the difference between AI and machine learning?

Machine learning is a subset of AI wherein machines apply knowledge from large amounts of data sets and perform tasks. Examples are speech and facial recognition or the computer that trained itself on a large data set of chess moves to beat the champion. (as opposed to the computer being dependent on rule based programming).

6. What is Bayes law or theorem?

It describes the probability of an event based on

prior knowledge of conditions that might be related to the event. It requires 3 terms: one conditional probability and two unconditional probabilities.

# 13 BlockChain Developer

*Blockchain technology allows digital information to be distributed but not copied and it isn't stored in a single location but is hosted by millions of computers simultaneously, accessible to anyone on the internet.*

1. What is a block?

A list of records with a hash pointer that acts as a link to the block prior to it.

2. What type of network must blockchain be used on?

Peer to peer.

3. What are some of the main characteristics of blockchain?

It is decentralized, it is publicly distributed, it has no single point of failure to shut down and is therefore very secure, it has the tremendous capacity of peer to peer network technology.

4. What is Ethereum?

An open software platform based on blockchain technology on which developers can build and deploy decentralized applications. It is not just a platform but also a programming language.

5. What is ether? It is a crypto token, a unique piece of code used to pay for transaction fees and services needed to run an application on Ethereum.

6. What is a smartcontract and how does it work?

It is a digital way to exchange something of value in a transparent and conflict free manner. An asset is transferred into a program and the program runs code to automatically validate a condition and then it automatically determines where the asset should go or if it should be refunded or if some combination of both should occur.

# 14 Cloud Engineer

*A Cloud Engineer or Architect is responsible for any technology duties related to the cloud. The cloud is software and services that run on the Internet, instead of locally on your computer. Most can be accessed through a Web browser and some via a dedicated mobile application.*

1. What are the 4 different deployment models of cloud computing?

Private, public, community and hybrid.

2. What cloud services are you experienced in?

As of this publishing the top 3 are AWS (Amazon Web Services) and Azure, which is Microsoft's version of cloud, and Google.

3. What are the layers of cloud architecture?

CLC or Cloud Controller, Walrus, Cluster Controller, SC or Storage Controller, NC or Node Controller.

4. Have you migrated any databases from onsite to the cloud and if so what databases and how did you do that?

An example of 2 ways would be: SQL to the cloud as a Service and SQL to an Azure VM (virtual machine).

5. Do you have any experience in platforms used for large scale cloud computing and if so, which ones?

There are 2: Apache Hadoop written in Java and MapReduce built by Google.

6. What cloud security aspects are you experienced in?

Listen for any of these words: identity management, access control, authentication, account provisioning, authorization.

7. What is your experience with multi-tenant cloud infrastructures?

A multi-tenant cloud allows customers to share computing resources in a public or private cloud. Each tenant's data is isolated and remains invisible to other tenants.

# 15 Mobile Developer

*Mobile Developers or Mobile Application Developers, specialize in writing software for small wireless devices such as smart phones and tablets.*

1. Do you have a specialty?
There are three main operating systems to consider: Apple's iOS, Google's Android (including its Amazon variant), and Microsoft's Windows and each has different associated technologies.

2. What are the main differences between desktop/web app development vs. mobile app development?

Different screen sizes and resolutions, variable connection speeds, battery consume, memory limitations would be some main ones....

3. Have you participated in the creation of any app that is available in the iTunes or Android stores?

If they have, get the names of the applications.

4. Do you have any experience migrating an application from one platform to another?

Most applications must be available on more than one operating system so reconfiguring or migrating and application is valuable experience.

5. How do you design user interfaces for mobile applications?

Responsive web design is to make each application or website appear as if it is specifically designed for that device and browser. For example, a specific widget or style sheet can be selected based on the device's screen size, resolution and aspect ratio. Each major device also has unique color palettes or icons as well as topography.

95958870R00026

Made in the USA
Columbia, SC
18 May 2018